FLY GUY PRESENTS: WEATHER

Tedd Arnold

Scholastic Inc.

For Nicole—T.A.

Thank you to meteorologist Scott Collis, and AnnMarie Anderson for their contributions to the book.

Photo credits:

Photos ©: cover tree & beach: lutherhill/iStockphoto; cover ocean: Sam Edwards/Getty Images; back cover: Jaim Simoes Oliveira/Getty Images; 4-5: Mount Washington Observatory; 6 top: Nadezhda1906/iStockphoto; 6 bottom: Media Bakery/Media Bakery; 7 top: Ariel Skelley/Getty Images; 7 bottom left: Comstock/Thinkstock; 7 bottom right: Elise Williams/eMarie Photography; 8: KingJC/Thinkstock; 9 top: zoran mircetic/iStockphoto; 9 bottom left: RobertHoetink/iStockphoto; 9 bottom right: William Thomas Cain/Getty Images; 10 top: Comstock/Thinkstock; 10 center left: Nickolay Stanev/Dreamstime; 10 center right: Tatyana_Mu/Thinkstock; 10 bottom: Maya Kruchankova/Science Source; 11: Daniel Sroga/Dreamstime; 12 top: Juhku/Dreamstime; 12 bottom: Vivian Mcaleavey/Dreamstime; 13 top: franckreporter/Getty Images; 13 bottom left: John Kirk/iStockphoto; 13 bottom right: Georg Gerster/Science Source; 14: Jaim Simoes Oliveira/Getty Images; 15 top: Welcomia/Dreamstime; 15 bottom: Slavenko Vukasovic/Dreamstime; 16 top: Picturetaker-Joseph/Thinkstock; 16 bottom: jefunne/Thinkstock; 17 top: Bill Sikes/AP Images; 17 center left: Michelangelo Oprandi/Dreamstime; 17 center right: Jonathan Fickies/Getty Images; 17 bottom: AP Images; 18: Clint Spencer/iStockphoto; 19: Tertius Pickard/AP Images; 20 top left: Amble Design/Shutterstock, Inc.; 20 top right: Tony Dejak/AP Images; 20 bottom: Planetary Visions Ltd/Science Source; 21: Jeff Schmaltz/DVIDS; 22 top: Jason Persoff Stormdoctor/Getty Images; 22 bottom left: Tatiana Morozova/Dreamstime; 22 bottom right: sshepard/iStockphoto; 23 top: NOAA; 23 bottom left: Sue Ogrocki/AP Images; 23 bottom right: Julie Dermansky/Science Source; 24: Darko Komorski/Dreamstime; 25 top: Roger Tidman/Science Source; 25 bottom: Oscar Perez, Casa Grande Dispatch; 26 top left, 26 top center: Dr. Scott Collis; 26 top right: David Parsons/iStockphoto; 26 bottom: yuancao/Getty Images; 27 top: Ida Mae Astute/Getty Images; 27 bottom left: Ryan McGinnis/Alamy Images; 27 bottom right: Jim Reed/Science Source; 28 top: Scholastic Inc.; 28 bottom left: greenviewphoto/Thinkstock; 28 bottom right: Jerryway/Dreamstime; 29 top: Macduff Everton/Getty Images; 29 center: Delstudio/Dreamstime; 29 bottom: Klein & Hubert/Nature Picture Library; 30 top left: Diane Bondareff/Bloomberg via Getty Images; 30 top right: Stephen J. Krasemann/Science Source; 30 center: Mandel Ngan/Getty Images; 30 bottom left: Madaree Tohlala/Getty Images; 30 bottom right: Mike McMillan/USDA; 31 top: Kali Nine LLC/iStockphoto; 31 bottom: Amble Design/Shutterstock, Inc.

ISBN 978-0-545-85187-9

10 9 8 7 6 5 4 3 2 1   16 17 18 19 20

Printed in the U.S.A.   40
First printing, 2016

Designed by Marissa Asuncion

A boy had a pet fly named Fly Guy.
Fly Guy could say the boy's name —

Buzz and Fly Guy were visiting a weather station.

"Whoa!" Buzz said to Fly Guy. "It's windy!
Let's get in out of the cold."

They headed for the door...

Weather is all around us, and it changes all the time. It affects what people wear and do each day.

When it is sunny, people wear sunglasses.

I wear sunscreen when I'm playing outside, too!

When it is cold,
people bundle up
in warm coats.

When it rains, people carry umbrellas.
They may even wear rain boots!

Earth's weather is controlled by the Sun. Changes in weather are caused by changes in Earth's atmosphere (AT-muhs-feer). Atmosphere surrounds Earth and is made up of air and water.

Our weather starts in outer space!

◦ BUZZ AND FLY GUY'S TIPS TO HELP EARTH ◦

1. Use less energy. Turn off lights when you don't need them.

2. Don't waste water. (Take shorter showers!)

3. Recycle!

4. Plant trees.

◦ **RECYCLING** ◦

◦ **PLANTING A TREE** ◦

Please help keep Earth healthy!

On Arbor Day, Buzz and Fly Guy
planted a tree. Then it started to rain.

"This is perfect weather for our
little tree!" said Buzz.

Buzz and Fly Guy could not wait for their
next field trip.

A tropical climate is warm and humid almost all the time! Humidity (hyoo-MI-di-tee) is a measurement of how full of water the air is. When the humidity is very high, fog and clouds can form.

A desert climate is dry all year. It almost never rains.

A polar climate is cold. There are summer days when it never gets dark and winter days when it is always dark. (Antarctica is both a polar climate and a desert climate!)

A climatologist (kly-muh-TAH-luh-jist) is a scientist who studies Earth's climates.

CLIMATOLOGISTS

Earth's climates are changing. Climate change can make the weather change, too. Global warming is melting glaciers, which adds more water to Earth's oceans. More water in the atmosphere may mean more big storms in some places and fewer in others.

MELTING GLACIER

FLASH FLOOD

FOREST FIRE

Some meteorologists tell people what the weather might be like in the future. This is called a forecast (FOR-kast).

METEOROLOGIST

Other meteorologists follow storms so they can better understand them. Some people call them storm chasers.

YIKEZZ!

STORM CHASERS

The climate (KLY-muht) is what the weather conditions are usually like in an area. There are four main climates: temperate, tropical, desert, and polar.

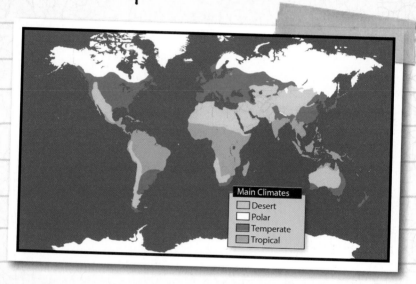

Main Climates
- Desert
- Polar
- Temperate
- Tropical

In a temperate climate, winters are cold and summers are warm.

summer

winter

When air moves, it is called the wind.
A breeze is a slow-moving wind.

Wind that moves quickly is called a gale.
A very strong gale can damage trees
and homes.

Three-quarters of Earth's surface is covered in water. Water moves between the ground and the air. It has three forms: liquid, solid, and gas.

liquid

solid

ice

snow

gas

When the Sun warms water on Earth, the water turns from a liquid to a gas. Then it rises into the air, forming clouds.

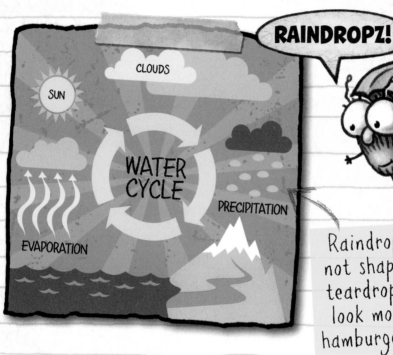

RAINDROPZ!

Raindrops are not shaped like teardrops. They look more like hamburger buns!

As the air gets cooler, the water changes from a gas back to a liquid or a solid. It can fall to Earth as rain, hail, or snow. This is called the water cycle.

Clouds form when water rises up into the air. There are different types of clouds.

Cirrus (SIR-uhs) clouds are wispy and thin and made up of ice.

○ CIRRUS CLOUDS ○

Cumulus (KYOO-myuh-luhs) clouds are fluffy and made up of water.

○ CUMULUS CLOUDS ○

These clouds look like cotton candy!

Stratus (STRA-tuhs) clouds are thick and flat. Fog is a stratus cloud on the ground.

STRATUS CLOUDS

Cumulonimbus (KYOO-myuh-loh-NIM-buhs) clouds are tall and gray and made up of ice and water. They are also called thunderclouds. They can cause heavy rains, lightning, or even tornadoes.

CUMULONIMBUS CLOUDS

Precipitation (pri-si-puh-TAY-shun) is rain, hail, or snow.

When water droplets fall back to Earth as liquid, they are called rain.

The colors of the rainbow are always in the same order!

If it rains too much, the ground may not be able to absorb the extra water. Water can pool in puddles. When puddles become large and cover a lot of land, this is called flooding.

FLOODED STREETS

If it doesn't rain enough, the ground becomes dry. When it doesn't rain for an unusually long period of time, it is called a drought.

DROUGHT

Sometimes winds make ice go up and down inside a storm cloud. Layers of ice stick to one another, forming balls. These ice balls are called hail.

Hail can be smaller than a pea or larger than a grapefruit!

If it is cold enough, snow crystals can grow inside a cloud and form snowflakes.

Every snowflake is different!

When it is very windy and snowy, this is called a blizzard. During a blizzard, winds can blow as fast as 45 miles per hour.

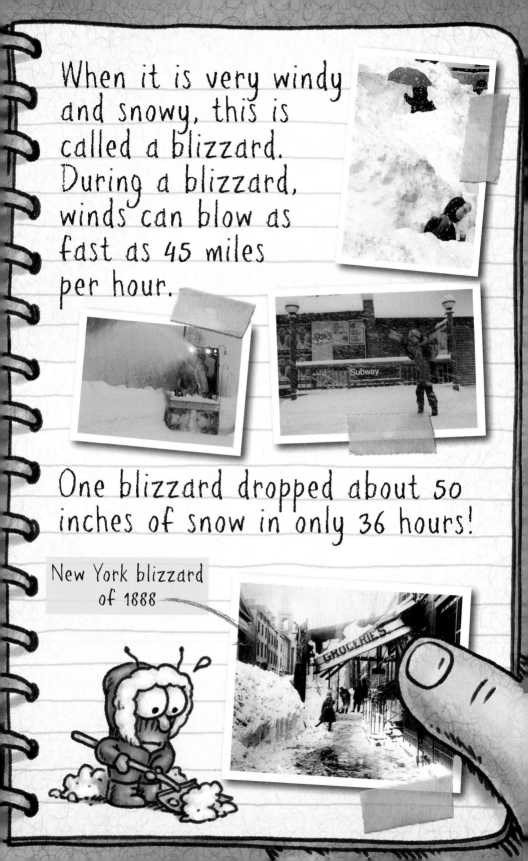

One blizzard dropped about 50 inches of snow in only 36 hours!

New York blizzard of 1888

Lightning is a giant electric spark. Electricity is created when water droplets freeze alongside rain and wind inside a storm cloud. The electricity builds up until it flashes outside of the cloud as lightning.

Lightning is hotter than the surface of the Sun! When it strikes, the air gets so hot that it makes sound waves vibrate. This creates a boom of thunder.

Lightning is dangerous!

TREE STRUCK BY LIGHTNING

Stay indoors if you see lightning. If you are outdoors, crouch down and stay away from tall objects.

**Remember:
When thunder roars,
head indoors!**

Hurricanes are the strongest storms on Earth. They bring heavy rain, high winds, rough waves, and floods to coastlines.

This storm has a different name depending on where it forms. In the Atlantic Ocean, it is called a hurricane. In the Indian and South Pacific Oceans, it is called a tropical cyclone. And in the North Pacific Ocean, it is called a typhoon.

A hurricane forms when a group of thunderstorms spins over warm oceans. As this group of storms becomes stronger, winds rush to its center. This causes the entire group to spin, forming one massive storm.

TYPHOON PARMA

From space, a hurricane looks like a giant pinwheel.

A funnel cloud can form when a powerful thunderstorm meets winds that change direction as they move up into the sky. If the funnel cloud touches the ground, it is called a tornado.

Tornadoes can do a lot of damage. They have some of the strongest winds on Earth. They can lift cows, cars, and even homes off the ground.

tornado damage

Tornado Alley in the United States has more reported tornadoes than anywhere else in the world.

People use underground shelters during tornadoes. If you hear a tornado siren, seek shelter right away!

underground shelter

Most tornadoes last for just 10 minutes!

Weather can get weird!

Tornadoes that form over water are called waterspouts.

A waterspout does not suck up water. But it can suck up frogs or other small animals. Animals can stay trapped in a cloud until they fall from the sky—like rain!

o FROGS o

o DUST STORM o

A black blizzard is another name for a dust storm.

A dust storm can happen when powerful winds blow across dry land. Clouds of dust and sand fill the air!

Meteorologists (mee-tee-uh-RAH-luh-jists) are scientists who study changes in weather. They use many tools.

Weather balloons and radar systems collect information about the atmosphere.

WEATHER BALLOON

RADAR IMAGE

RADAR

A wind vane shows which way the wind blows.

WIND VANE